Clean Freak and Other Stories

Lindsey M. Costley

Lulu Enterprises, Inc.
3101 Hillsborough St., Raleigh, NC 27607

"The Test" also appears in the July 2009 issue of *Northwest Literary Review*.

Author's note: The events described in these stories are real. Some characters have fictitious names and identifying characteristics.

ISBN 978-0-557-06873-9

Contents

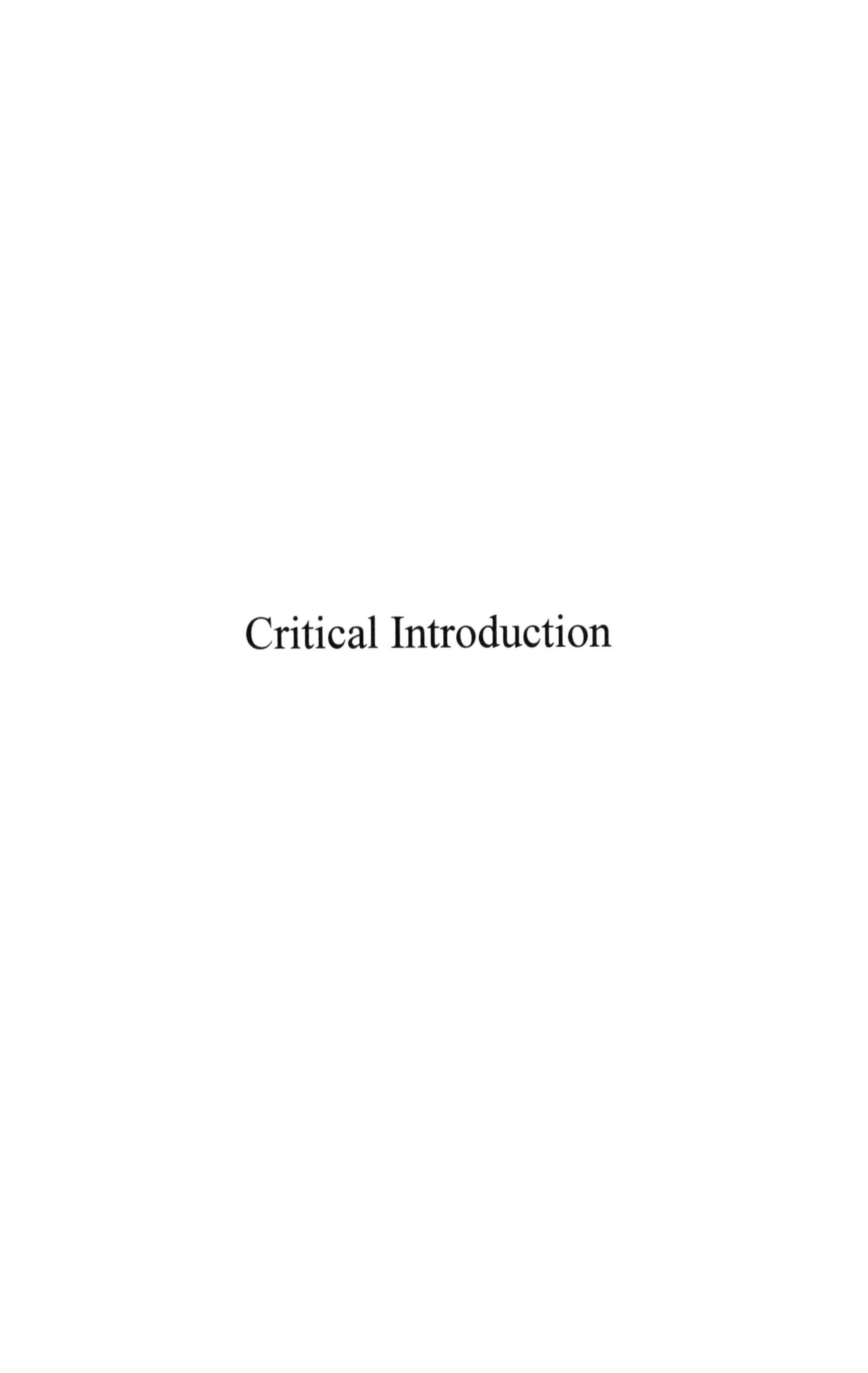

Critical Introduction

The Funny Thing Is…

I write because I have been raised by storytellers. When I was little, I remember crowding around the dinner table on holidays to hear my grandmother and her siblings share stories about growing up after the Great Depression. The stories were always the same, but everyone listened like they were listening to a collection of my grandmother's greatest hits.

My grandmother would begin with the story about the pet goat her family had for milk and the day she and her siblings tied it to a tree in the hills while they went to play for hours. While they were gone the goat walked in circles around the tree until it strangled itself. They knew Baca, my great-grandmother, would kill them all if she found out they were responsible for the goat's death, so they buried it in the backyard at the house. Except they didn't dig the hole deep enough. The goat had already stiffened and so the legs stuck straight out of the ground like four furry, flowerless plants. Baca couldn't miss it. When she returned to the house the children told her the goat ran away. Then she looked out the window.

It has always been my favorite story. Over the past several years I have learned to tell my own stories. To improve my humor, I turned to the experts.

When I first read David Sedaris, I immediately knew nonfiction was where I belonged. I loved his work and I read everything I could get my hands on: *Naked*, *Dress Your Family in Corduroy and Denim*, *Holidays on Ice*, *Barrel Fever*. I began to study Sedaris in order to make my own humor better. I thoroughly examined "SantaLand Diaries," "Jesus Shaves," "Dinah the Christmas Whore," and several of my other favorites in an attempt to understand why they were funny. Aside from the interpersonal relationships that were inherently funny, Sedaris uses hyperbole and telling nicknames for his minor characters that describe them in a humorous manner. His delivery is spectacular; the timing is perfect. Even if I sense the punchline is coming, it happens at the perfect moment when, no matter how many times I have read or heard a particular story, I still laugh out loud.

Periel Aschenbrand uses similar devices in her book *The Only Bush I Trust is My Own.* For Aschenbrand a key element of her humor comes from repetition and dialogue. The style of Aschenbrand's writing is unique in that her presence is stronger than that of others, like Sedaris. I truly admire the voice of her writing—the persona conveyed in her writing—and I strive not to have a similar persona, but to create myself as a unique character, clearly identifiable within the page.

Aside from reading humor, I also watch a lot of standup comedy. The delivery of a routine that is recited is different than the delivery of material that is to be read, but this examination still betters my own writing. From watching standup—not all of which is good—I have learned the art of telling a joke. A joke cannot be forced. Comedians who consistently flop tend to work really hard to get to the joke itself; they spend so long on the setup that when they finally arrive at the punchline, the crowd groans because it wasn't worth the build-up. The setup has to appear effortless.

Standup comedy has also helped me to read my work aloud. The difficult thing about reading to an audience is the group mentality: often, people will laugh at a certain point in a story depending on the reaction of others in the room. I always have my suspicions about where my listeners will laugh and I am prepared to pause accordingly, but I never plan on soliciting the reaction in case it doesn't happen where I expect or it happens where I don't expect it. I would like to say that studying this phenomenon in greater depth would provide me with a foolproof formula, but I don't think that's really possible. No matter how long someone has been a standup comedian, some nights just don't go as well as others.

It wasn't until the end of my college career that I truly learned what it means to revise a piece. Before, all I did was edit my pieces: I corrected spelling errors, grammar malfunctions, and added small points of clarification. Then I took a course with Lara Vesta. Lara explained that revising is re-visioning a piece; there may be a salvageable gem within the original document, but revising involves cutting large portions and expanding in new directions. Now, I revise.

I label the older version of an essay about my moderate to severe obsession with cleanliness "Clean Freak v 1.0." Any editing earns the piece a new title of "Clean Freak v 1.2" or "Clean Freak v 1.5." When the essay undergoes actual revisions, I create a new blank document on my computer, which I title "Clean Freak v 2.0." The first version is copied and pasted into the new blank document where I can experiment with any number of things while having the security that version 1.0 is fully intact elsewhere on my hard drive. If I am completely unsatisfied with the new direction of a piece, all I have to do is erase the contents of the document and begin again.

Of course, most pieces go through more than one revision, so I have a file labeled "Old Versions" where I place all of the outdated materials. The contents of this folder show the progression of a piece from its most primitive stage all the way through a point of relative completion.

I call my writing nonfiction and I believe it to be nonfiction, however, I agree with author Jack Driscoll when he says, "If a story is completely true, it's probably not that great of a story anyway." It would be fair to say that all of the stories included in this collection are true. The questions lie in whether the events happened in the order I say they did, involving the people named, when I claim they happened. Some events may be embellished. Some are stories I have heard, but when it comes down to the stories themselves, it doesn't make any difference what I witnessed and what I only heard about. All I will say is that every event I write about can and could have happened exactly as I wrote it to happen. The stories you are about to read are real events experienced by real people. In the end, it doesn't matter what is wholly true and what is partially fictional, because the things no one could ever believe are the things that happen to me every day.

Clean Freak and Other Stories

Clean Freak

I open the freezer door and remove the package of chicken breasts. Using an inverted Ziplock bag like a glove, I grab two, simultaneously turning the bag right side out. The chicken never touches my skin as I close the bag and submerge it in warm water. I carefully inspect my surroundings for small bits of chicken ice that could melt and leave germy specs behind.

Once the breasts have thawed, I label one hand the salmonella claw—usually my left hand. I use the salmonella claw to touch the chicken while my right hand holds the knife to cut off any excess fat or bone. Only the blade of the knife touches the chicken. I balance the knife on the thin ledge betw-een the two sinks while I rinse the chicken with cool water before placing it into the pan. The claw grabs the Ziplock bag, filled with the excess tissues and chicken water, and carefully lowers it into the waste bin. I use my right hand to spray soap onto the salmonella claw and turn on the faucet. Then I wash both hands together for at least sixty seconds.

While the chicken cooks in the oven, I wash both basins of the sink, any utensils that have been used in the process, and all surrounding areas of countertop. I then microwave the sponge on high for one minute to sanitize it. Now my housemates are free to enter the kitchen when they please. They may touch whatever they would like. The kitchen is safe.

You can learn a lot about a person by watching him or her clean. There is a noticeable difference in the ways of people who clean because they know they should clean and people who clean because they desire cleanliness. My mother cleans because she craves cleanliness. From the moment I was old enough to do chores, I received a detailed list of instructions:

1. *Floors are not to be washed with mops.*
    a. *Mops can easily breed bacteria and mold because the average person does not take care to strain fully and dry the mop after use.*
    b. *Floors are washed with a rag.*
2. *A rag that is used on the floor is not used on the tables.*
3. *A rag used in a bathroom is never used in another part of the house.*

4. *Rags used for cleaning are washed together in a separate load from all articles of clothing.*
    a. *The same goes for floor mats or rugs.*

The list was posted inside the door of the cabinet where a majority of the cleaning supplies were stored. There were also lists detailing which cleaning solutions were to be used on which surfaces, proper water-to-cleanser ratios for different solutions and desired cleanliness, instructions for cleaning biohazard-caliber spills or accidents, and a foolproof order in which the chores should be done so as not to spread germs from dirty rooms into rooms that have already been cleaned.

I was a young sponge who soaked up all of my mother's fears and obsessions. I was terrified of being dirty. My mother tells me I have always hated to be sticky. As an infant, I would whine and raise my hands for her to wipe them clean. Most of all, I hated to have food or other sticky substances on my face. At restaurants, I grab more napkins than I could ever use because each napkin has a threshold before it stops cleaning and starts wiping stickiness back onto my skin.

My earliest memory is running through the grass at my cousin's old house when I was three. I was chasing someone and stumbled awkwardly, stepping in a loaf of raccoon shit the size of a large burrito. I instantly froze in place, staring at the horrors below me. The loaf swallowed my entire foot and shoe. I could feel its inner warmth through my Keds. Tears welled in my eyes. I raised my face to the heavens and bellowed. Those shoes were instantly dead to me. I didn't even want my foot anymore.

My aunt bleached my foot until my skin started to peel and then we went home. Dad carried me to the car because I refused to walk on my soil-ed foot.

My father once told me I would never go to a movie theater again if I knew how much fecal matter was on the seats. Ever since, I immediately change my clothes when I return home after seeing a movie. Every article of clothing is instantly placed in the dirty clothes hamper. I wash my hands. Depending on whether I was wearing long or short sleeves, long pants or shorts, I sometimes shower before I allow myself to sit on any furniture.

Some believe my father only told me this to torture me, but he behaves exactly as I do after returning from a movie. I wouldn't be surprised if more people behaved this way. After all, stories of fecal matter on movie theater seats aren't simply urban legends. News reporters in almost every state have ventured to movie theaters to swab seats, headrests, armrests, and floors. In every case, the bacterial cultures have shown an alarming amount of fecal colonies. I'm not typically one to believe everything I hear on the nightly news, but with such consistent results, I am forced to think about what I could contract every time I sit in a movie theater seat. Then, of course, I have to wonder whether the germs I run into on a daily basis are any worse than the occasional trip to the movies.

For several summers, I worked as a counselor at a summer day camp. Tuna Fish Hands was six years old when I first had him in my group, and every day he would bring a Starkist Tuna Kit for lunch—the kind with the fresh-sealed pouch of tuna, not the can. A six-year-old kid does not have the kinetic ability to open the fresh-sealed pouch and scoop out the tuna with the doll-sized spoon offered in the kit itself, so Tuna Fish Hands would scoop it out with his bare hands. And then he would eat it with his bare hands. All the while smiling at me while tiny morsels of tuna collected in the corners of his mouth. Had tuna been dyed red, Tuna Fish Hands would have painted himself a large clown-like grin at every meal.

Every day I offered Tuna Fish Hands my napkin from my lunch and every day he would graciously accept it. But other than the initial exchange, he never once touched it during the course of his meal. And then Tuna Fish Hands would touch me on my shoulder or back and ask if I would read to him after lunch leaving that particular spot of my body to smell like tuna for the rest of the day. Eventually, I started bringing a change of clothes so I could sit in my car comfortably on the drive home after work. Tuna Fish Hands would insist on holding my hand when we walked to pick out a book and then he would touch the book and point at the pictures leaving microscopic remnants of spitty tuna on each page.

My least favorite period of time was when Tuna Fish Hands started to bring little canned sausages for lunch. He would ask me to open the can for him, which I could never do without some of the juice spilling on either my hands or some other part of my body and then he would eat them with his fingers and drink the remnants of the sausage water that was left in the can. I almost vomited the first time I witnessed this act. I also decided I preferred when Tuna Fish Hands had tuna for lunch.

I would like to think that my level of cleanliness will help me to lead a long life with no major illnesses, but my odds aren't great. I know too many individuals like Tuna Fish Hands who will most likely give me the bubonic plague or salmonella and then I will die in agony of dehydration as a result of dysentery. I just hope I can make it through the week; I still need to clean the kitchen and the bathroom.

The Test

They probably thought they had just witnessed a murder.

They sat, stopped at the red light, as the garage door opened and a dark figure ran out into the dim lighting to start the silver Honda parked in the driveway. After starting the car the figure opened the back door and ran back into the dark mouth of the garage. Two figures reappeared, dragging a large mass between them. In the dim light provided by the floodlight atop the garage, the witnesses might have seen a dark stain forming along the floor of the garage—a trail of blood following the figures to the backseat of the Honda Accord.

The two figures took several attempts to lift the large mass into the backseat. Every time the light turned green, the audience quickly vanished. Not once did anyone stop and offer help. If they called the police, we were gone before they arrived.

It was late in the summer; the rain lasted longer. The nights were darker. My sister and I were each home from college—Leslie from her third year, me from my first. We dined alone in front of the television—Mom at work, Dad in various stages of completing various chores.

The news reported flash floods on the northeastern side of Colorado Springs. The sliding door opened; my father stumbled forward, both hands clasped tightly on his head as lightning cracked through the darkness behind him and thunder shook the house. Blood mixed with rain streamed down his forearms and off his elbows onto the cream-colored carpet. Without taking another step, my father fell, face first, onto the living room floor.

Our eyes met briefly as my sister and I looked up from where our father lay. Without saying a word, I got onto the floor, trying to roll him onto his back. Leslie ran to the kitchen to grab towels and ice. In the time it took me to roll him over, Leslie returned with her second trip of towels.

After searching through his bloody, black hair we found a large L-shaped gash about two inches above his hairline, the center of which was white. We took turns asking, "Dad, can you hear me?" as we pressed cold towels on his forehead and applied pressure to the wound. Leslie tried tapping his cheeks, shoulders, and chest, but received no response. "He has a pulse," she stated as if we were EMTs, "but I don't think he's breathing."

"We need to move now. Ambulance?"

"No, it takes them too damn long to get here. Lift on three." On my sister's count, we tried to lift the man I could barely roll over on my own. Two hundred and thirty pounds feels like a hell of a lot more when he isn't moving and when he's your father.

Dad used to be a firefighter in the Air Force, so Leslie and I have been First Aid Certified since we could sign our own names. This has been extremely beneficial living on the busiest corner in our neighborhood. Lately, emergency response teams don't arrive fast enough. Even though the local fire department is only a few blocks away, they never arrive before the unit located halfway across town.

Accident after accident, my father is always the first one out the door. Leslie and I run out after him. Mom always calls for emergency units. The accidents test our education. Dad asks us what to do before we reach the edge of our front lawn. We learn in real time. We act quickly. We can't risk being wrong.

I can only remember one accident when Dad yelled, “Stay inside,” before we had even reached the front door. We tried to watch from the bay window on the west side of the house, but all we could see was a practically flattened VW Bug and our father, covered in the blood of people he had never met.

When he came inside hours later, his whole body trembled. I could hear his muffled cries through the heater vents while he showered. Leslie and I knew not to ask any questions.

This is not your father. This is different. He is everyone else.

Dad always told us that if he were ever the first to arrive on the scene of an accident in which he knew the victims, he wasn’t allowed to help them. He could administer care until another unit arrived, but he would have to step away once it did. I never understood why. I always assumed that I would be of more help if I had a personal connection to the people I helped. I thought I would want to help them more. I thought I would care more about the outcome.

I didn't understand that I wouldn't be thinking rationally through my emotions. I didn't understand how dangerous a personal connection could be. We should have called for help, but we were afraid. We didn't think anyone could help him better than we could. So we did it alone. We didn't call for backup. We didn't wait for another unit to arrive.

Out of the fear that we would drop him if we were able to lift him, we decided to drag our father by his armpits, keeping his head elevated. Once we made it down the step into the garage, Leslie ran to start her car—there was no way we could lift him high enough to put him into my Jeep or his Chevy truck.

It took three attempts before we could get his body into the backseat. We struggled to bend him in a way that he was both upright and inside the doors. Leslie held a towel on his head while I sped through the canyon to Memorial Hospital.

When it comes to medical emergencies, Dad is always calm under pressure. Of course, it is his job to be calm. If he is ever worried or afraid, he never allows it to show.

He cut his hand open on the meat slicer at our family's restaurant one morning. He was cleaning and in a moment of carelessness, ended up with the circular blade in the center of his hand. Before removing his hand from the machine, he reached over to grab a clean towel off of the shelf. He slowly removed his hand and then immediately wrapped it in the towel, using his teeth to tie a large knot on top of his hand. He clenched his wounded hand in his opposite armpit and made his way to the office.

My grandfather, practically deaf at this point in his life, was reading the newspaper in the office. Papa frequently lost his glasses atop his head or in the front pocket of his shirts, but it's not like he could see any better with them on. Knowing his chances of making it to the hospital were better if he drove himself, my father hollered over the kitchen noise and told Papa he had to run an errand. After hearing no response, he drove himself to the hospital and returned with a fistful of stitches. Papa never noticed he was gone.

"Are you going to have to shave a chunk of my hair?" my father asked the doctor.

"That shouldn't be necessary with the staples, Mr. Costley."

"No, but... even though it isn't necessary, my daughters would really appreciate it if you shaved a chunk of my hair. I owe them something to laugh about." Dad continued his effort to repay us with some humorous token for an evening we could never forget, but the doctor did not see things the way we did.

We left the hospital hours later. Dad's hair was matted where the seven staples held his head together. He looked as though he were wearing barrettes, assembled in an L-shaped part in the center of his head. Even without a shaved chunk of hair, I laughed every time I caught a glimpse of him in the rearview mirror.

When we returned home, the rain had stopped. We walked onto the deck in the backyard where my father pointed to the metal water-meter box. There were thick black hairs on the corner. "The rain was coming down so hard that I ran over here. I was trying to duck under the ledge to get out of the rain and I hit my head on the bottom edge of this meter. I must have hit it pretty damn hard, because I thought I could make it inside to clean up, but I passed out before I could even close the door behind me," my father explained.

"We noticed," I laughed.

"Look at this mess," he gestured toward the bloodstained carpet, "Looks like it's set pretty good. We may have to get new carpet."

"Mom's going to be so mad at you."

"Yeah."

"She's going to laugh when she sees your head though," I said.

"Who wouldn't?" Leslie joked.

As terrified as we had been, we knew we could never tell him, but we also knew he understood. I could see it in his eyes when he looked at us. He was thankful. He was proud. We had passed the ultimate First Aid test. We were ready to leave his care and live in the world on our own. Our laughter broke through the silence of everything we would never say.

Deaf at Twenty

The curtain opens to thunderous applause. I can barely hear Sam's voice as he yells, "Two, three, four," and breathes in tempo, raising his trumpet to his lips. The horns open the show with a blaring lick that cascades into the beginning of Blood, Sweat and Tears' "More and More." The amplifier at my back shakes the stage under my feet and I fear I might fall through at any given moment. Through the blinding lights I can see the house is full. Next show my monitor will have to be a little louder; I can barely hear Thea sing.

Ever since my days touring Colorado as a bassist for multiple bands ranging in style from grunge-punk to funk to neo-classic rock complete with rippin' horns, I have had poor hearing. Too many nights spent in crowded spaces with loud amplifiers and raucous feedback beating my eardrums have led me to moderate deafness. I can still hear; I'm just limited to a lower range of pitch.

Naturally, I managed to find a woman who absolutely despises repeating herself. Somehow we make it work. I say, "What?" often or I just nod at her blankly until she figures out I have no idea what is going on, then she eventually gets so frustrated with trying to make herself audible that she says, "It doesn't matter anymore." Hours later, I piece together the fragments of words to realize I had the choice between pumpkin or cherry pie for dessert. "Oh, pumpkin would be—" my statement trails off as she gives me a look that could have cooked the pies faster than our ancient oven. "Actually, I'm not that hungry."

My hearing fluctuates so often that it doesn't seem like a worthwhile expenditure to buy hearing aids right now. I still hear fairly well. Some days my hearing is great. My condition needs to be much worse before I seriously consider hearing aids. Hell, my grandmother just got hers and she has been almost completely deaf for the past five years.

At Christmas the entire family was together, sharing stories over dinner; one of my young cousins was telling a story about something that happened at school and every person was turned to face her. Then, in the middle of my cousin's story, Grandma said, "Did you hear about that Cindy Brinkley? She's getting a divorce from that cheating husband of hers." All eyes turned to Grandma.

"Even if you can't hear, can't you at least *see* that we are all looking at someone else and that her mouth is moving!" my mother said. "And it's *Christie* Brinkley, damn it!"

"What?" Grandma replied, genuinely surprised. "Was someone talking?"

I was honestly a little upset when I found out that my grandmother started to wear hearing aids. I thought our family gatherings would be so much less amusing without the constant misunderstandings that occurred.

My hearing loss is not nearly as severe as my grandmother's, but it still bothers me. I don't think it would matter to me as much if I were older, but I'm in my twenties. Old people are supposed to have bad hearing, not me. I keep hoping if I take a long enough break from performing music my hearing will eventually come back. I haven't had much luck yet.

I have trouble understanding people on the phone. The tiny speaker can never be loud enough for me to understand the person on the other end unless I happen to be somewhere as quiet as a morgue. And I can't hear shit in an airplane. God forbid we ever had to make an emergency landing and follow the verbal instructions to dislodge some part of the seat while breathing through the magical sack that falls out of the flight attendant's hand. Luckily, my troubles with flying occur before I ever reach the plane.

Aside from a rare situation in which I spent almost forty-five minutes in the line to get into security screening because the woman checking my ID didn't believe I was the same person with bleach-blonde hair and no corrective lenses pictured in my driver's license, I typically don't have problems with airport security. Traveling to visit my parents for spring break, I noticed there was going to be a problem when my bag kept going in and out of the screening machine. There was something perplexing about my carry-on luggage but I could not hear what the two Transportation Security Administration workers were saying to each other about my things. I quickly tried to run through the list of items packed in my bag that could resemble potential weapons.

A woman wearing white latex gloves grabbed my bag and then paused before removing it from the screening machine to ask me a semi-audible question. I tried to piece together the fragments I heard before she would confiscate my bag and leave me trapped in Portland. Parade? No. Hand grenade? God, I hope not. I continued to stare at her blankly while I searched for the proper phrase.

Before I could finish, another TSA worker tapped me on the shoulder. "Is the-at a hear-ring ay-ed?" she asked me in a slow, loud voice that clearly annunciated each syllable.

"Yes!" my face lit up at the thought of escape. I had no idea what the hearing-aid object was but I knew the proper response would send me on my way in time to catch my flight.

I later discovered when I unpacked my luggage that I had forgotten to remove the earpiece for my metronome from my backpack before I left. My girlfriend is convinced that it is a sign from some higher power that I should wear my "hearing aid" at all times.

Maxwell's Silver Hammer

I knew it was stupid. I knew it was wrong the second the idea left his smirking lips and I got that sick feeling in my stomach.

"Costley, you've been worrying your whole life," he joked with his usual half-grin.

I thought carefully about my next words, "Fine, but I'm going with you," as if my presence was all the protection he needed.

Max and I lowered ourselves, inch by inch, into the warmest hot spring along that stretch of the

Colorado River. We sat, submersed in heat, until our bodies adjusted to the temperature and the water started to feel lukewarm.

"Ready to lose?" he asked.

"That's what you think."

"On three. Nikki's count."

I nodded in agreement and readied myself for three.

It's a cold climate thing. Some call it "Polar Bearing." The most extreme cases involve cutting a hole in a frozen lake and then diving into the lake nude. The most common version involves hot tubs in winter: one who accepts the challenge must leave the warmth of the hot tub to stand outside in the cold or roll around in the snow. The objective is to stay in the cold for as long as possible. The average person lasts less than ten seconds. Max had a longer challenge in mind. It was a race—from the hot springs to the lap pool, under the frosted tarp that covered the pool, from one side to the other and back, then up the rocks and into the hot springs.

On three we scrambled out into the early December air and ran, our bodies steaming, to jump into the frozen waters of the lap pool. The sharp rocks cut my feet as I ran, but slipping was a better fate than losing to Max. I was first to the pool, but Max was close behind. I dove into the water and felt the thin layer of ice break around my fingertips, clearing the way for my body to follow. The water was so cold it took half my breath away. I tried to focus on my form: streamline with three big dolphin kicks and then into a modified breaststroke. My chest hurt as I prayed for the wall to come soon. I gasped for another breath at the wall, "Cheating!" Max would have yelled if he had seen me in the darkness. I turned and swam back, pulled my slippery body out of the pool, ran back up the rocks—cutting my already bloodied feet—and cannonballed into the hot spring.

"I win! Ha! Take that!" I yelled. Our friends and beloved spectators cheered. "Ha! Did you hear me? I win, Max!"

Silence. "Max?" Louder, "Max!"

Nothing.

Spectators and friends ran with me back to the pool. I crashed through the small chunks of ice, punching my way through, trying to find him in complete darkness. He had to be under the tarp. "We can find him," I yelled. "We have to find him."

When we found him it was too late. Max didn't take a breath at the wall like I did. He didn't cheat. He drowned beneath the tarp.

Max's mother answered with panic in her voice, accustomed to late night phone calls, but knowing that no call coming in at three in the morning would bear good news. I could overhear her sobs while she talked to the Police officer. I could have stopped him. I should have stopped him. I knew it was stupid. I knew no good would come of it. Max was always making me do this shit, ever since we were little.

"Swim to the bottom of the pool and try to pull off the drain cover," he egged me on over fifteen years ago.

"You first!"

The difficulty of Max's challenges progressed as we got older. They started to involve bets, "I bet you can't do a back flip off the guard shack!" and wagers, "I dare you."

"Watch me!"

Our dares became less public when Max was a lifeguard at the pool. We would wait until nightfall and then return with our friends to do can-openers, centerfolds, Mammy Yokems, and flying squirrels off of the buildings that surrounded the small community pool.

Max would do anything.

One summer he broke his foot in an attempt to jump off the guard shack, land on the diving board like a trampoline, and launch himself into the pool. The impact of the stiff diving board shattered the bones in his foot and he fell to his knees on the diving board before tumbling off the side into the pool. I dove into the pool and pulled his lanky, screaming body out of the water.

"That was probably one of the dumbest things I have ever seen you do," I laughed.

The emergency room personnel took one look at me, still dripping in my swimsuit with a towel wrapped around my waist, then at the shirtless Max, balled in fetal position, then outside into the hot summer night. "Isn't it a little late for swimming?" the nurse remarked.

Seeing Mary Stark for the first time, I cried so hard I could barely stand. "I'm so sorry," I whispered as she held me close. "It's all my fault."

"Lindsey Costley," she ignored my apologies, "I remember those ridiculous swimsuits you wore every summer. The wetsuits. God, you looked ridiculous. I remember the first time we saw your band play. Max said, 'Mom, that's Lindsey Costley,' and I couldn't believe it. It had just been so long. You know, he thought you were just the coolest chick alive."

If I hadn't been crying hard enough before, I lost it then. "He was a great person, Mary. I'm so happy to have known him." It wasn't worth apologizing again.

I would say I miss Max, but "miss" doesn't cut it. I can "miss" a phone call and call the person back. I can't call Max back. I can't make up the time he has been gone. I can't make up for his loss. It's hard to know that I won't see Max every summer at the Little Dipper Pool. Sometimes he was a real pain in the ass and I hated him for it, but I remember more good times than bad. He captivated audiences with his humor and wit. He amazed me with his art and his poetry. He is one of the reasons I continue to write. At the Maxwell Silver Memorial Lecture at Ft. Lewis College in Durango, Colorado, his mother told me, "Write, write, write. Every day. It's your job to tell his stories for him."

Every so often I look to the skies at night and the Little Dipper shines through in the brightest white. I know no matter how far I am from Max and our childhood memories, I can always go home and be surrounded by his energy. Then I wake up to the most magnificent sunrise.

Happy Halloween, Mom

From what I can remember, Halloween was always a big deal. It was the time when my mother could exert her crafty superiority over other mothers by creating the ultimate Halloween costumes for my sister and me. She always made our costumes, sometimes it was necessary to purchase accessories, but for the most part she did it all.

The first Halloween I can remember, I was a pumpkin. I remember the itchy pillow stuffing and the light reflecting strips that were sewn into alternating sections of my orb shape. The suit was large enough for me to wear my snowsuit underneath. Growing up in Colorado, every Halloween costume had to be planned around winter gear, unless your costume was Man/Woman with Hypothermia.

My mother says the best Halloween was the year that I was Davy Crockett, but she only prefers that year because at one of the houses we went to, an old woman asked me who I was and I told her my real name instead of who I was dressed as. It's not my fault she didn't phrase her question correctly. She wanted to know who I was and so I told her. Had she wanted to know who I was pretending to be, I would have said Davy Crockett. Although my mother loves this story, the actual best costume ever was my clown costume in fourth grade. Even the makeup was spectacular. She stitched the multicolored jumper out of random fabric she found in the house and I wore a pair of my father's throwback Nike sneakers. No one at school recognized me.

The costume creativity of my peers started to die-off in junior high. Girls started to care more about having a cute costume than having a *good* costume. It only got worse in high school. The focus became more on Halloween being the one day they could violate the dress code. Nikki Haskell went as a Victoria's Secret Angel freshman year. She sat in front of me in English. She was not wearing pants. Or clothes for that matter. Bra. Panties. High heels. Wings. And a furry halo. I was Axl Rose, of Guns 'N' Roses, that year. Had I been the anatomically correct Axl Rose, I probably would have had an erection in the middle of English class.

The only time I had a lame costume was my freshman year of college. Halloween kind of snuck up on me. I was so focused on doing well in my classes that I didn't really consider what my mother had done for me since the beginning of time. It takes a lot of effort to make a good costume. I would like to think I have redeemed myself though.

One year I made my own crab costume. My mother mailed me some parts and a hot glue gun, but other than that I did it all myself. The following year, I was Robin, Boy Wonder, with no assistance from my mother.

I take tremendous pride in having a good Halloween costume that I didn't buy previously assembled. Other women my age tend to favor the slutty over the creative but that's not what Halloween is about. If they would just look around they would see they could get much more attention with a good costume than they do as just another whorish angel among the masses.

At the end of the night, I can feel proud to show my mother the pictures of Batman and Robin from Halloween '07. I have not failed her.

Skinny

I have always been skinny. Actually, that's not true. I can only remember being skinny, but I weighed almost nine pounds when I was born. I looked like a Butterball turkey, but I thinned out once I was able to walk.

I have inherited my mother's high metabolism. During periods of intense physical activity I cannot eat enough to fully replenish what I am burning. But I sure as hell try. People who know me don't comment too much on my weight because they know—or assume—I exercise. My mother never used to work out, but she has recently started a regimen of core strengthening exercises. Her exercise is geared more toward being active than achieving a certain body image or type. In that sense, her exercise is atypical.

My mother looks absolutely ridiculous if she has to run for any reason. I have only seen her run once in my entire life: I can't remember why, but she ran from her bedroom to the living room of our house. It was the most unnatural movement I have ever seen a human being make. Her arms and legs flailed in slow motion while her body unevenly bounded forward. I have never seen her run since then and I doubt I ever will.

I am broader than my mother, however she stands a few inches taller. I believe that she technically weighs more than I do, but she has absolutely no muscle. Her calves are straight. Not thick straight, but missing-a-calf-muscle straight. Her arms have a similar twig-like quality. She is the single most uncomfortable person to cuddle up to when you are having a rough day. She has no cushion whatsoever, just pointy, sharp joints. But her embrace is special because it is wholly her own; I have never loved a pointy hug as much as I love the unchanging characteristics of my mother's.

I wasn't aware of her frustrations with skinny until middle school, when girls began to care more about body types and self-image. Skinny sucked. Other girls started to say things like, "You're so skinny!" with a hint of disgust. Any time they commented about my stature it was always a negative thing. There was always a huge aggravated sigh followed by, "You're just so small," or, "I bet three of you could fit inside my jeans."

I didn't want to be skinny, it just happened. I wanted to be normal so they would stop picking on me all the time. It didn't feel good to be called small or skinny or thin when they said it. The way they said it, it had the exact same tone as someone saying fat-ass, but had it been fat-ass someone would have flipped out and notified the administration. Then every student would be forced to attend a seminar about why we can't call someone a fat-ass and hurt her self-image, but calling someone toothpick-skinny is totally all right.

At a bar one night, this woman walked in and ordered a Skinny Bitch, which visibly puzzled the bartender and so she clarified, "It's just Diet Coke and vodka." The bartender chuckled and replied, "How fitting." *How fitting*. I was surprised he thought it fitting since skinny people are not the targeted market for diet sodas. I was also surprised she didn't take offense to the label given her by a complete stranger. And I was utterly stunned when he scolded me for ordering a Fat Bitch—a regular Coke with vodka.

Then, I was watching TV with my mom one day and there was some show on with the main goal of trashing celebrities because that makes us feel better about ourselves or some bullshit. And this analyst of celebrity-ness or something comes on like the authority on weight talking about how Nicole Richie is such-and-such height, weighing blah-blah-blah pounds, and that is completely unhealthy by all medical standards, and she would know because she's on fucking VH1 talking about someone who has done absolutely nothing important with her life. And I realized that I am the same height and weight as Nicole Richie.

So really all of these people talking about how disgusting and unhealthy she looks… I look like that? Jesus, I hope not. My thighs touch when my feet are shoulder-width apart, but isn't that normal? She has no thighs. I think, *Maybe it's just the pictures*. Technology has given us the ability to alter any image to fit the ideal or perpetuate the concept of what is ideal, regardless of whether the person pictured naturally fits this same ideal.

When people talk about skinny and fat, they associate numbers with these terms. They decide the spectrum within which we consider someone to be unhealthily skinny or dangerously overweight, but body weight is complicated and healthy weight is very specific to every individual. A far better determination of what is and isn't healthy considers all of the factors that contribute to one's health (height, weight, body fat percentage, eating habits, activity levels, etc.). We can't assume any individual weighing 105 lbs. is unhealthy just as we can't assume any individual who weighs 250 lbs. is fat.

People just don't get it. They censor themselves before they say fat because fat is a loaded word. They can't say fat because fat is offensive to fat people. But they can say skinny, twiggy, thin, and anorexic (as a descriptor) as much as they want without even considering the way they say it. Why can't they just say fat and skinny with the same inflection as *average*?

It's about body image. We are trained to want to have the ideal and some people practically kill themselves to obtain it. So when it comes easily for others we are conditioned to hate those people because they don't have to work as hard to maintain the ideal. The problem is not the people who don't have to work for it. The problem is the ideal. There should not be one concept of what beauty is. We should not all strive to be the same because the differences are what make people beautiful. Who determined what the ideal image is? Not me. I know too many people who don't fit the ideal who I consider to be absolutely gorgeous, no matter their size.

Thoughts at Thirty Thousand Feet

In the past few years, I have become a seasoned veteran of the wonder that is air travel. I have experienced everything from the world's smoothest landing imaginable to digging my nails into the armrest and praying that each drop wasn't going to bring me into the mountainside.

When I flew for the first time, I was very young and had never imagined falling to my death from thirty thousand feet. These fears appeared soon after September 11th. For a time I paid close attention to the dramatic display of emergency information offered by the flight attendants and followed along closely in the cartoonish emergency card.

Then the fears went away. I started to think rationally about the number of flights that land every day in comparison to the ones that don't. My odds of dying in a plane crash are low enough to never consider. But I still do. Before we have responsibilities, we don't have to think about things like plane crashes, but as soon as we have responsibilities—a pet, a partner, a family, a business—we think about every risk we take, no matter how small, and the impact these risks could have on others.

I hate that I find myself boarding every flight, praying for Papa, Uncle Tony, Max, and Amy to look after me and get me home safe. But I think even more than hating the fact that I ask for this safe passage, I hate the comfortable, relaxed feeling I immediately feel after my prayer. I don't dislike relaxation, but it shakes my agnostic worldview to achieve this relaxation through prayer. Even if it is prayer to loved ones lost and not necessarily some higher power. Agnostic or not, every time I board a plane, it makes me feel better to know that I am in their hands.

My days of paranoia allowed me to memorize all of the pre-flight safety information, so now I can always zone out and begin my reading instead of watching the safety play performed by the flight attendants. In the event of a real emergency everything they tell us would go to hell, anyway. People would be screaming, throwing loose objects, and pushing each other out of the way as they ran for the nearest emergency exit. In the event of a water landing, remember to grab the seat cushion, which is infested with someone else's farts and clutch it to your chest. I would rather take my chances at treading water, but if you really want the fart cushion you may help yourself to mine as well.

On some flights, the seatbacks contain tiny television screens where you can choose to pay eight dollars for a movie or five dollars for twenty-six channels of Direct TV. Or you can watch the free map of the trip, like I do. The map shows the plane in relation to the flight path as well as the altitude and speed at which you are flying. It's pretty fancy.

Near the end of one flight, I was watching my favorite free channel, which told me we were two thousand feet away from the ground, when the woman next to me pulled out her emergency card and started fanning her face like her life depended on it. I glanced over to see that she was as red as the inside of her wide-open mouth and sweating like she threw her four-ounce drink on her face. Naturally, the first thing that came to my mind was: oh, shit. By this time, all I could do was stare out the window and wish we were still at an altitude where I would have been allowed to use my portable electronic device to mask the sounds of her vomiting. I could only hope that I wouldn't puke if she did. But we were almost on the ground. Buck up, lady. Tough it out. We could see the landing strip from the window.

And then she blew.

She violently heaved into the little white sack while her husband pretended not to know her and I focused on the view out the window, imagining my reaction if a speck of vomit happened to land on my arm. I'd probably smack the barf bag into her vomit-covered face, then sanitize for a few hours and take a bath in bleach when I arrived home. Or I could just cut my arm off. Her vomit scent filled the recycled air around my face and I decided it would be best to hold my breath until the air got sucked back into someone else's breathing space.

When we landed two seconds later, I couldn't look at her. I was embarrassed for her, embarrassed that she couldn't hold on for just one minute. She had been fine the whole flight until the very end. Our landing was smooth. Everything about the descent was perfect: no turbulence, no big drops in altitude, no barrel rolls or loop-de-loops. What was wrong with this woman?

At the same time I was pleased. Pleased because my puker waited to puke until the very end. After all, it could have been far worse. She could have started during take-off, and then I would have had to sit next to her as she filled bag after bag with her vomit, cycling her vomit air through the plane over and over again, until eventually I, too, would be sick. And then it would have been a miserable occasion for everyone.

Blind Date

Even though I was comfortable with my lesbian identity, I didn't date much in high school—at the time, I was the only openly gay student in the entire school. If for some reason my friends were able to find another lesbian, they instantly tried to set us up with each other, saying, "She's perfect for you!" She was never perfect. On some occasions she wasn't even a lesbian.

Instead of thinking about the qualities and characteristics typically used to align two people, my friends used one determining factor: lesbian. It doesn't make any sense to me to believe that all lesbians are perfect matches. It's like this: when I meet a random heterosexual male, I don't say, "Oh my God! I know someone else who is heterosexual; you absolutely have to meet my friend [insert hetero-sexual female name here]! You're perfect for each other!" Except this is exactly what my heterosexual friends did to me time and time again. Eventually, I gave up on denying every lesbian they met.

An acquaintance tried to set me up on a blind date with this girl she knew someway somehow. Looking back I don't know how I was acquainted with Lyra. She was another lesbian and the friend of a friend, but I can't for the life of me remember who, which probably should have been my first red flag.

Lyra called my house and told me she wanted to set me up with this other lesbian she knew: Brandi Carlisle. I didn't even know Lyra; she knew nothing about me or what I was looking for in another woman. It bothered me that not only my heterosexual friends assumed this was the only criteria needed in finding me a quality partner, but Lyra, one of my kind, made the same assumption. Yet I was a desperate fifteen-year-old lesbian living in Colorado Springs, Colorado, so I jumped at the offer with little hesitation.

Lyra said she and her girlfriend would pick me up and we would go bowling. Like the dweeb I was, I responded, "I love bowling!" which is not something you should openly admit if you ever want to appear cool.

On the day of the blind date, I anxiously waited for Lyra's dark blue Volkswagen Jetta to pull into the driveway. When Lyra arrived with her girlfriend—whose name I can't remember—I went to sit in the backseat of the car, catching a quick glimpse of myself in the window before I opened the door. Only, the image in the window was not my reflection; there was a girl sitting in the backseat of the Jetta. A girl who I mistook to be my own reflection.

"Oh sorry, I'll go around to the other side," I said. After I closed the door I stood in the same spot, wondering how obvious it would be if I ran back into my parents' house. I didn't want to be rude, so I walked around to the other side and got into the Jetta.

Brandi Carlisle looked exactly like me. Now, most people use "exactly" in a frivolous manner and thus the word no longer bears any significance, but Brandi Carlisle was my doppelganger. At the time, we had the same bleach-blonde hair, crew-cut and spiked with gel. We both wore glasses with thick black frames. We wore men's clothes. She was roughly two inches shorter than me, but we had a similarly thin physique.

We are often mistaken to be the same person. Years later, we have each changed in the same ways. She allows her hair to be its natural light brown color, but cuts it shorter than she used to. She also wears hair gel less often. Family friends who frequent the restaurant she works at always say they saw me working there. They swear by it. Every time I assure them I would never work there, have never worked there, and I know exactly who they speak of. And every time they swear she's me. If for some reason, they believe she isn't me, then they are convinced we should date. Who, aside from true narcissists, would ever want to date someone who looked exactly like him or her?

At the bowling alley, Lyra proceeded to publicly display her affection for what's-her-name. Their mouths were open so wide, a person from five lanes away could have seen their tongues wrapping around one another's in a swirl of saliva. I was left sitting awkwardly next to Brandi, staring at the lesbian couple across from us, praying Brandi didn't want to do anything they were doing. I focused on bowling. Since Lyra and what's-her-name were rarely paying attention, I often bowled during their turns just to shorten the period of time I would have to sit in agony watching them drown each other in saliva. I scored almost 200, which was really good for me. Brandi scored less than 100. She was awful.

When I finally grasped Lyra's attention in the rare chance that her eyes were actually open, she saw it was time to leave. I couldn't wait to get home. As soon as Lyra pulled into my driveway, I already had my seatbelt unbuckled and my door half open. “Wait!” Brandi called, “Can I get your number?”

“Uh… Lyra has it.” I closed the door and quickly walked up the driveway and inside my parents’ house.

As much as I thought I would learn my lesson from the experience and never agree to be set up on another blind date, I repeated my mistake. Twice.

I am a Woman, Too

"Excuse me, I believe you're in the wrong restroom," she said as I walked in the door, barring me from entry.

"Oh, am I? How embarrassing. These signs are just so confusing because they put the picture of the person wearing a dress here and then the picture of the person wearing pants there, and I haven't worn a dress since my mother could dress me—well there was my aunt Tina's first wedding when I was eight, but—well I just figured I would follow the words printed along the bottom. This one says 'Women' and I do have two X-chromosomes, a fully functional vagina—complete with a uterus, ovaries, and fallopian tubes—and protruding breasts. Maybe what they should do is create a third bathroom with the picture of the person wearing pants and the word 'Women' along the bottom for people like me."

Or at least that's what I wish I would have said.

Instead, I apologized and walked away from the department store bathroom. If it had been the first time, I might have ignored her and walked in anyway.

I'm a woman. Other women are no better than me simply because they appear more feminine; now, they may be better than me for other reasons, but they don't get an instant-win card just for looking the part. Do they think I'm stupid? Why do they assume I cannot read or discern between symbols when I walk into a public restroom or locker room?

For this very reason, I would rather piss my pants in public than enter a public restroom. I tell people I am afraid of the germs, which isn't a complete lie, but it's not my main deterrent.

Being rejected from a public restroom simply because I don't look feminine enough is the most degrading thing that has ever happened to me. And it happens often. The worst part is when I'm with friends who yell at my attackers; the attackers yell back, "Well it's her fault for dressing that way! If she didn't want me to think she was a boy, why would she dress like that? Why would she cut her hair so short?" Because I don't like the way women's clothes fit me. Because I was ugly when I had long hair. Because I was uncomfortable and awkward in my own skin.

Who dictates what women are supposed to look like anyway? What would happen to the world if men's and women's fashions were interchangeable? I doubt it would explode. Maybe for once in world history, we would be breaking the boundaries of a hetero-normative society. And I would be considered normal. For once in my life, I would be normal.

I am no different than anyone else. I worry about money. I worry about what the hell I am going to do with my life. I want to be loved. Eventually, I want to raise children. I want to be able to support a family. I want to travel someday. I want to be happy.

I am a woman. I don't look like you, but I am a woman, too.

The Penis

The model entered the art studio unannounced, his face visibly dirty, moustache unkempt. He looked practically homeless. "Oh, thank God," I said quietly, "He's wearing clothes."

The student to my left laughed to himself before replying, "Not for long," and, "Don't worry, they're never attractive."

My face probably expressed my mind's panic, but I tried to appear calm. Though the course syllabus said the corresponding unit for this particular week involved models, it said nothing about the models being actual people. It also said nothing about the models being nude. The professor gave no indication that we were in fact drawing a nude model. He simply began class by saying, "We have a model today." Judging by my classmates' facial expressions, I was not alone in my surprise.

When the model reappeared from behind the curtain in the corner of the room, he was wearing the same bathrobe my father has. It was a terrycloth robe with black and red plaid. Once he was wearing my father's robe, I started to notice other similarities, like how his hair was parted. The color seemed only a shade lighter. The skin tone of his chest looked similar. "Oh, shit," I whispered as the model approached the small stage in the center of the room. In one quick motion, he dropped the robe to the ground.

I winced and closed my eyes. *He is not your father. He just has the same robe. Get over it.* I took three deep breaths in through my nose and out through my mouth, shook my shoulders, through my arms, all the way to my fingers. I slowly opened one eye, afraid of what I might see, before I decided it was safe to open the other. I strategically repositioned my easel, both to add to the length of time I was not drawing the model, and to serve as a shield to protect me from his nether regions.

For the first several poses, his back was to me. His hair was matted and greasy. His back was covered in acne and random patches of coarse black hair. This man had hips. I have never seen a man with hips. The curve of the line looked almost like a female figure until I got to his ass. His ass was wrinkled and sagging. I had never seen a rear end that looked like that, but I imagined his to be what my ninety-year-old grandfather's ass would have looked like.

"Change pose," my professor instructed and the model turned to face me.

I ducked behind my drawing board as though he was firing a weapon in my direction and it was the only barrier that could save me. Hidden behind the easel, pretending to sharpen my pencil and clean my kneaded eraser, I waited to regain my composure.

When I looked up at the model I noticed he appeared physically ill. He was sweating and the color of his face was a slight olive green. His shoulders swelled with each heavy breath he took. Sweat was pooling in the crease between his large breasts and gut. I couldn't smell him from where I was positioned in the room, but I imagined he smelled sickeningly sweet. Like rotten fruit. I tried to wipe away the disgusted look I could feel forming on my face. I didn't want him to feel any more self-conscious than I assumed he already felt.

"Change pose," my professor called again from the back of the studio.

The model asked, "Do you want me to try something more splayed-out?"

Splayed-out? Absolutely not! Nothing splayed-out! My heart beat furiously inside my chest fearing the worst pose I could have ever imagined. I thought of him lying spread-eagle with his hands behind his head, his hips thrusting forward in an awkward accentuation of his man-parts.

I don't know why, but my professor must have agreed that splayed-out was an acceptable position. The model turned his back to me to assume the splayed-out position. He lowered himself onto all fours and for a brief moment, I saw his asshole before I jerked my head to the right, meeting the eyes of the student next to me.

"I think I just saw what you saw," she said almost in a state of shock.

I nodded and swallowed hard to prevent myself from gagging. Up until this point I wouldn't have believed anyone if they told me there was something more horrific than the sight of this man's pock-marked bare ass. And then I had seen it.

When I was sure he had fully completed his transition from standing to splayed-out. I peered around my easel at the model lying on the floor. His position was awkward and unnatural. I assumed it was more the pose of a disfigured dead body than someone relaxing on a beach or lounging on a sofa.

I did everything I could to avoid looking at his penis. All of my drawings were of his awkwardly positioned torso. Eventually the professor looked over my shoulder and advised me to draw the whole male figure. I sat for awhile, staring at the page filled with flabby torsos and sagging ass-cheeks, contemplating whether the whole male figure could look any worse than what I had already seen. So I looked and what I saw was extremely disappointing.

The penis before my eyes caused the corners of my mouth to turn down in a scowl. It was smaller and floppier than I had expected. I had pictured something more like a banana covered in skin. The penis was buried in a forest of curly brown hair. And I had no idea why anyone would keep one or desire to have one. It was completely unsanitary.

Because it was so small and hidden by so much hair, the penis was a rather unnoticeable part of the whole male figure. It could almost go unnoticed on the page, even in the splayed-out position.

Awkward position after awkward position, I began to wonder where the hell they even found this guy. We were supposed to practice drawing the human form in different poses that we could later incorporate into our other drawings. Aside from standing perfectly still with his arms at his side or sitting on a crate with his hands on his knees, I don't think I saw him do anything I could incorporate elsewhere. His poses sucked. *Splayed-out* was only one in a host of completely unnatural poses he decided to display for our viewing pleasure.

I assumed this must have been his first nude modeling gig, which partially explained why he looked so sickly toward the beginning of class. How does one find out about nude modeling? Is there a special section in the classified ads: *Desperately Seeking Nude Models*? That could be dangerous. Then again, it would probably produce no worse than my homeless-looking-father's-robe twin.

Session after session, I became more and more comfortable drawing the model. I came away from the class with several drawings I am proud of, none of which are a result of the model's awful poses, and my father gained a new, solid blue bathrobe.

Acknowledgements

Sara: I can never truly express how grateful I am to have you in my life. You are so wonderful and you have helped me in every step of this process: living the stories, telling the stories, revising the stories, formatting the stories, etc. Thank you. I can't wait to begin our story. I love you always.

My family: Dad, Mom, Leslie and Randy, Grandma, Grandy, Cindy and Dale, Nick, Rachel, Tina and Rob, Jacob, Caroline, Casey and Suzie,

Ashlen, Landen, Wade, Grandad and Martha, and all who extend beyond. Thank you for all of your support through the years, I really hope you don't hate me after reading this book. And I'm sorry if you didn't know I was a lesbian before. Surprise!

Robin, Kristen, and Nana: thank you for always making me feel like family.

My friends: this would be an epic if I listed each and every one of you by name. You know who you are and you know that you matter in my life. Some of you may even recognize yourselves in these stories. Consider this my tribute.

Steve Schriener: I am a writer because of you. I will teach because of you. You are a dear friend and mentor and I hope to always have you in my life.

Doyle Wesley Walls: you have refined my writing ability beyond comparison. I am lucky to have been one of your students.

All of the faculty at Pacific University, the English Department, and especially Darlene Pagán, Pauline Beard, Mike Steele. Thank you for your knowledge and guidance. I am the person I am today because of all of you.

My classmates. Thank you all for reading my work and providing feedback over the past several years. You are a talented group of writers, and I consider myself fortunate to have studied with you.

And you: thank you for reading this book. I hope you have enjoyed every minute of it. And if you have, tell your friends about this book. Buy them a copy for their birthdays.

Photo by: Denise Giesbers

LINDSEY M. COSTLEY was raised in Colorado Springs, Colorado. Lindsey received her Bachelor of Arts in Literature and Creative Writing from Pacific University (Forest Grove, Oregon) in May 2009. She and her partner currently reside in Mesa, Arizona where Lindsey continues to write and work.

www.ingramcontent.com/pod-product-compliance
Ingram Content Group UK Ltd.
Pitfield, Milton Keynes, MK11 3LW, UK
UKHW020237250726
13967UKWH00001B/414

9 780557 068739